Spiritual Journeying

An exploration in the light of Spenser's
The Faerie Queene and 'Attār's
Conference of the Birds

Imam Monawar Hussain

Copyright © 2016 Imam Monawar Hussain

All rights reserved.

Published by The Oxford Foundation, Clarendon House, 52 Cornmarket Street, Oxford, OX1 3HJ, United Kingdom

www.theoxfordfoundation.com

Email: info@theoxfordfoundation.org.uk

ISBN: 1539898660
ISBN-13: 978-1539898665

TO THE KNIGHTS

CONTENTS

	Acknowledgments	i
1	Introduction	3
	Chivalry	4
	Allegory	6
2	Islam in English Literature	10
3	The Faerie Queene	14
	A Vision of Gloriana	14
	The Redcrosse Knight	15
	'Armour of God'	17
	House of Holiness	22
4	Conference of the Birds	26
	A Vision of Sīmorgh	29
	Sheikh Sam'ān	32
	The Greater Jihād	34
5	Conclusion	40
	Bibliography	43

ACKNOWLEDGMENTS

This work was originally submitted in partial fulfillment of the requirement of a Master of Arts degree in Abrahamic Religions at the University of London. I am most grateful to the following for their support during my study at Heythrop College, University of London - Mariann Jakabb, Dr Ahmad Achtar, and Dr Michael Kirwan SJ.

And of course, gratitude, thanks and love to my family and friends.

Wa mā tawfīqī illā billāh.

1 INTRODUCTION

From a very early age I have been fascinated with spirituality. In particular, how the different religious traditions envisage the human beings spiritual journey to God? This dissertation reflects very much my own personal journey of discovering how two of the world's Abrahamic traditions - Christianity and Islam – address this question. I shall seek to do this through exploring two texts, the Elizabethan chivalric romance epic by Edmund Spenser (1552?-1599)[1] entitled, *The Faerie Queene*[2] and a Sūfī text by Farīd ud-Dīn 'Attār (1142?-1220?)[3] entitled, *The Conference of the Birds (Mantaq at-Tayr)*.[4] Why choose these two texts? I have chosen these for

---

[1] There is disagreement as to his date of birth. Brink has argued that based on Spenser's school and university records his date of birth is likely to be 1554 rather than 1552 as others have asserted. See Jean R. Brink, 'Revising Edmund Spenser's Birth Date to 1554', *Notes & Queries*, 56 (2009), 523-527.

[2] Edmund Spenser, *The Faerie Queene*, ed. by A.C. Hamilton (Harlow: Pearson Education, 2007). All quotations of the poem thereafter from this book are in the format Book, Canto, and Stanza.

[3] There is disagreement as to the date of his birth and death as well as spuriousness of some of the works attributed to him. This discussion need not detain us, suffice to say that the work subject of our exploration is authentic and acknowledged to be the work of 'Attār. See H. Ritter, "Attār', in *Encyclopaedia of Islam, Second Edition*, <http://referenceworks.brillonline.com/entries/encyclopaedia-of-islam-2/attar-COM_0074> [accessed 21 July 2016].

[4] Farīd ud-Dīn 'Attār, *The Conference of the Birds*, trans. by Afkham Darbandi

two main reasons. Firstly, both are shaped by the chivalric ideal for virtuous perfection, with both texts employing the idea of the journey as a didactic plot and this enables both authors to address the human being at the deepest spiritual level; Secondly, both are masterpieces in allegory and impregnated with multiple meanings. That is to say that they provide a map of how the human being, fallen, cut off from her origins – might once again regain that which was lost at the fall – God. Both texts are rooted within the religious cultures in which they were given birth but nonetheless speak beyond their contexts, hence their enduring appeal and relevance.

My treatment of the two texts will not be exhaustive due to the limitation on space, but it will be focused. With reference to *The Faerie Queene*, I will examine the Redcrosse knight's symbolism of the 'armour of God' and his sojourn in the house of Holiness. I find the 'armour of God' intriguing, as it transforms the clownish young man, an upstart, who seems to have no experience of combat or anything remarkable about him into 'the goodliest man in al that company.'[5] What is the significance of the symbolism of the armour of God? What does it signify to the individual Christian on the path to God? My primary focus in the *Conference of the Birds* will be on the Sheikh Sam'ān story, this seems to give its fullest articulation to 'Attār's key teachings on the Sūfī aspirant's path to God.[6] In the remainder of this introduction, I shall outline below the two common strands between the two texts, that of chivalry and allegory.

CHIVALRY – THE SEARCH FOR VIRTUOUS PERFECTION

In his letter to Sir Walter Raleigh (1554-1618), Spenser states that his aim 'of all the booke is to fashion a gentleman or noble person in virtuous and gentle discipline.'[7] 'Fashion' here means to 'train; mould, create' a noble virtuous person.[8] He is not thinking here of a secular gentleman but a Christian one. The armour ascribed to this noble person is, Spenser informs us, drawn from Ephesians 6.11-17; we shall explore this later, when we examine Redcrosse knight closely. Doyle rightly, makes the point that Spenser's 'contemporaneous readers were Anglicans of one height or another, a fact which means that they were Christians and that, like Christians in general (of that era), they thoroughly knew and accepted the teachings of the Gospels and St. Paul and St. Augustine.'[9] The Knight in

---

and Dick Davies (London: Penguin Books, 1984).

[5] Spenser, *Faerie Queene*, p. 717.

[6] 'Attār, *Conference*, p. 57-75.

[7] Spenser, *Faerie Queene*, p. 714.

[8] Spenser, *Faerie Queene*, p. 714.

the sixteenth century, as depicted in much of the Elizabethan and European literature, is a metaphor for the Christian man, who goes on an adventure - a quest for 'perfect virtue'.[10] Spenser is therefore drawing on a long literary tradition, in the words of Morgan:

> There is nothing unconventional or unorthodox in the combination of holiness and chivalry that Spenser presents in the 'Legend of Holiness'. Chaucer's ideal of knighthood in the portrait of the Knight (CT, A 43-78) is focused on holiness, for the Knight's campaigns are all religious campaigns and they are fittingly set in the context of a pilgrimage. Piety is given exceptional emphasis in Sir Gawain and the Green Knight as the final virtue of the final group of virtues... Thus by beginning The Faerie Queene with the virtue of holiness Spenser writes from within a well-defined romance tradition...[11]

This idea of chivalry and the chivalrous quest for virtuous perfection is not dissimilar to the tradition of *futuwwah* in the Islamic tradition. The word *futuwwah* is not found in pre-Islamic Arabic language but the root from which it is derived, *fatā* (pl. *fityān*) meaning 'young man' is.[12] It conveys a sense of youthfulness, courage, valour in battle and generally a chivalrous person. During the early Islamic period this idea of the *fatā* was integrated and transformed into the Islamic chivalric ideal (*futuwwah*) through the teachings of the Qur'ān and *aḥadīth* (sing. *ḥadīth*) and took its inspiration from the exemplified lives of the Prophet, his companions, the Ṣūfī masters and the past Prophets, especially Abraham, Joseph and Jesus.[13] This aspect of the Islamic tradition has also been defined as the greater Jihād and we shall return to this when we examine the Sheikh Sam'ān story in chapter four.[14]

---

[9] Charles Clay Doyle, 'Christian Vision in *The Faerie Queene*, Book 1', *College Literature*, 3 (1976), 33-41, (p. 34).

[10] Norman Council, 'Ben Jonson, Inigo Jones, and the Transformation of Tudor Chivalry', *ELH*, 47 (1980), 259-275, (p. 259).

[11] Gerald Morgan, 'Holiness as the First of Spenser's Aristotelian Moral Virtues', *The Modern Language Review*, 81 (1986), 817-837, (p. 822).

[12] Ibn al-Husayn al-Sulamī, *The way of Sufi Chivalry*, trans. by Tosun Bayrak al-Jerrahi (Vermont: Inner Traditions International, 1991), p. 20.

[13] Muhammad Ja'far Mahjub, 'Chivalry and Early Persian Sufism', in *The Heritage of Sufism: Classical Persian Sufism from its Origins to Rumi (700-1300)*, ed. by Leonard Lewisohn (Oxford: Oneworld, 1999), p. 551-553.

The purpose of the greater jihād is to battle against one's selfish and lowly desires, to reign them in, so that one's whole being is modelled on virtue. The man eminently recognised as the perfect embodiment of chivalry in Islam was 'Alī, the fourth caliph of Islam.[15] Resit has defined *futuwwah* as, 'rebellion against all evil and striving for a sincere servant-hood to God. [..] *futuwwah* is a composite of virtues, such as benevolence, munificence, modesty, chastity, trustworthiness, loyalty, mercifulness, knowledge, humility and piety.'[16] The key idea was that each 'young man' carries within him innate noble qualities, these needed to be nurtured and fully realised under the supervision and training of the Sūfī master. The core training was to engender 'complete and utter selflessness' so that the 'young man' placed others before himself through 'unlimited generosity' both through charitable giving but also 'generosity of mind and character.'[17] Hence *futuwwah* from the very beginning was an intrinsic part of Sūfīsm.[18] Sūfīs claimed spiritual lineages connecting them back through a set of Sūfī masters to the Prophet. Mahjub notes that this was achieved through the master, from generation to generation, handing down to a disciple a 'dervish cassock' (*khirqa*). The same applied to the Sūfī Chivalric Orders whose 'lines of affiliation were traced, without exception, back to the Prophet's son-in-law, 'Alī ibn Abī Tālib, establishing him as the supreme source of the virtues of futuwwah.'[19]

ALLEGORY

Spenser uses allegory or what he terms as 'continued Allegory, or darke conceit'[20] to realise his aims in *The Faerie Queene*. Whilst

---

[14] Shaykh Muhammad Hisham Kabbani, *Self-purification and the State of Excellence* (California: As-Sunna Foundation of America, 1998), pp.43-44.

[15] Resit Haylamaz, *Ali Ibn Abi Talib: The Hero of Chivalry* (New Jersey: Tughra Books, 2011).

[16] Haylamaz, p. vii.

[17] Ines Asceric-Todd, 'The Noble Traders: The Islamic Tradition of "Spiritual Chivalry" (*futuwwah*) in Bosnian Trade-guilds (16th-19th centuries)', *The Muslim World*, 7 (2007), 159-173, (p. 160).

[18] Husayn Wā'iz Kāshifī Sabzawārī, *The Royal Book of Spiritual Chivalry*, trans. by Jay R. Cook (Chicago: Kazi Publications, 2000), p. 2. For a good introduction to Sūfīsm, see, Carl W. Ernst, *Sufism: An Essential Introduction to the Philosophy and Practice of the Mystical Tradition of Islam* (Boston: Shambhala Publications, 1997).

[19] Mahjub, *Chivalry*, p. 552.

acknowledging that some might find the idea of the allegorical devise unpleasant and would rather employ sermons or precepts, he nonetheless settles for allegory. 'Attār too employs allegory and this is a very common practice in much of Sūfī literature as it enables the author to impregnate the text with deep allegory, thus giving birth to an ocean of meaning, each seeker quenching her thirst in accordance with her spiritual attainment. This is no surprise, for allegory as a literary tool has an ancient history. It has been used from the Greco-Roman period and was an excellent devise both for the author but also for the reader, who could interpret the allegory in many different ways, thereby giving the text an enduring appeal.[21]

Mitchell[22] has argued that both the Old and New Testaments were understood as texts shaped through a twin process. Firstly, that they were written in compositional allegory, which means that the authors took the view that meaning would be taken from outside the text, secondly, that the texts would be open to an allegorical reading, irrespective of whether the author had intended that. She argues that in this instance Jesus is considered the 'compositional allegorist' and St. Paul as the 'allegorical interpreter'.[23] The New Testament is full of Jesus' parables that can be interpreted in many different ways and in examples such as Mark 4 vv.3-9, are offered a commentary later by Jesus in vv.13-20. She does also suggest that in the modern era, this theory has been questioned and one of the primary criticisms has been that it is a foreign pagan accretion onto the Christian understanding of scripture. I take the view that an allegorical interpretation does not necessarily preclude a literal interpretation and that a combination enriches our understanding of the text. Augustine, one of the great figures of Christianity, suggests in his Confessions that when a literal rendering of a text seemed 'perverse' he would 'unveil' it through a spiritual understanding.[24] Hagen suggests that in the medieval and reformation

---

[20] Spenser, *Faerie Queene*, p. 714.

[21] For a thorough treatment, see 'Allegory', in *Encyclopedia of the Bible and Its Reception*, <http://www.degruyter.com/view/db/ebr> [accessed 28 August 2016]. See also, John S. Pendergast, 'Christian Allegory and Spenser's "General Intention"', *Studies in Philology*, 93 (1996), 267-287, in which he discusses Augustine's exegetical method to show how 'Augustine's method may have broadly influenced sixteenth-century allegorical invention' (footnote, p. 272).

[22] Margaret M. Mitchell, 'Allegory', in *Encyclopedia of the Bible and Its Reception* (Berlin: De Gruyter, 2010), 793-800.

[23] Mitchell, *Allegory*, p. 793-795.

period a fourfold interpretative method was employed known as the quadriga. This was 'history, allegory, tropology, and anagogy.'[25] As an example, taking these categories in the same order, Jerusalem was understood as meaning the city, the church, the human soul and heaven. Of course, the reformers, such as Luther, Erasmus and Calvin, rejected this interpretative method but for our purposes what is significant is that one of the giants of European literature, Dante, advocated the use of the same method to understand his classic, *The Divine Comedy*. There is also gathering evidence, that it is inconceivable that Spenser was not influenced by Dante's work.[26] The multiple levels of meaning and Dante's interpretative method has been articulated well by Lings:

> The idea of different meanings existing simultaneously at different levels, however strange it may seem to us, was altogether familiar to men of letters throughout the Middle Ages and even later – witness Spenser's The Faerie Queene... According to Dante, 'writings are to be understood and should be expounded chiefly according to four meanings' or in other words the literal meaning should be considered as a veil over three others, which he specifies as 'allegorical, moral and anagogical.[27]

Allegory in the Islamic tradition, was also found at a very early stage, through influence of Persian literature but also from verses of the Qur'ān (e.g. 18:10-12 and 18:65). Al-Ghazālī has argued that in addition to the literal interpretation of the Qur'ān, there are other levels of esoteric meanings.[28] Friemuth notes examples from the works of leading

---

[24] Mitchell, *Allegory*, p. 799.

[25] Kenneth Hagen, 'Allegory', in *Encyclopedia of the Bible and Its Reception* (Berlin: De Gruyter, 2010), 800-802 (p. 800).

[26] Mathew Tosello, 'Spenser's Silence about Dante', *Studies in English Literature, 1500-1900*, 17(1977), 59-66. See also, Anne Paolucci, 'Women in the Political Love-Ethic of the *Divine Comedy* and the *Faerie Queene*,' *Dante Studies, with Annual Report of the Dante Society*, 90 (1972), 139-153. Paolucci argues that there are 'substantial parallels' between the *Divine Comedy* and the *Faerie Queene*.

[27] Martin Lings, *The Secret of Shakespeare: His Greatest Plays Seen in the Light of Sacred Art* (Cambridge: Quinta Essentia, 1996), p. 14.

[28] Nicholas Heer, 'Abū Hamīd al-Ghazālī's Esoteric Exegesis of the Koran', in *The Heritage of Sufism: Classical Persian Sufism from its Origins to Rumi (700-1300)* ed. by Leonard Lewisohn (Oxford: Oneworld, 1999), pp. 235-258 (p. 256-257).

philosophers and Sūfīs utilising allegory as a means of articulating their teachings on wisdom, virtue and the soul's journey to God. In particular, the Prophet's *mi'rāj* (nocturnal journey to the heavens) resulted in a huge wealth of allegorical treatises.[29] This event, more than any other, was to ignite the spark in great Sūfī masters to produce some of the greatest allegorical masterpieces in world literature. The *mi'rāj* became the prototype for treatises on the soul's love for and journey back to God. Schimmel in her masterful work on Sūfism states that 'Attār's *Conference of the Birds* 'is the most perfect poetic introduction to the mystical path.'[30]

Bruijn has cited one of the earlier Persian works from the eleventh century by the poet and lexicographer Asadī. This is a chivalrous novel written for a local ruler in Azerbaijan but for our purposes what is important is that the author utilises allegory and it contains strong religious elements. The thrust of Asadī's allegory is that 'man is permanently threatened by oppressive armies of demons, that is by the forces of the passions generated by his lower soul.'[31] These he argues can only be overcome through the aid of religion and wisdom. Bruijn argues that Asadī's work provides a good example of the development of the *mathnawī* literary tradition, through Sanā'i and 'Attār, that eventually culminated in Rūmī's magisterial *mathnawī*. He notes that Sanā'i's second major work, was a *mathnawī* that utilised allegory describing his own spiritual journey, with much of it dedicated to his Sūfī master.[32]

To recap then, both of the texts are grounded in chivalric virtue, employ allegory and the journey as a didactic tool.

---

[29] Maha Elkaisy Friemuth, 'Allegory', in *Encyclopedia of the Bible and Its Reception* (Berlin, Boston: De Gruyter, 2010), pp. 807-808 (p. 807).
[30] Annemarie Schimmel, *Mystical Dimensions of Islam* (Chapel Hill: The University of North Carolina Press, 1975), p. 306.
[31] J. T. P. de Bruijn, 'Comparative Notes on Sanā'ī and 'Attār', in *The Heritage of Sufism: Classical Persian Sufism from its Origins to Rumi (700-1300)*, ed. by Leonard Lewisohn (Oxford: Oneworld, 1999), pp. 361-380 (p. 366).
[32] Bruijn, *Comparative*, p. 367.

2 ISLAM IN ENGLISH LITERATURE

In his excellent summation of works on Islam in English literature, Masood makes the point, that on first account, the two may seem as distinct disciplines but he suggests that the volume of studies produced over the last century would 'justify speaking about Islam and English literature in the same breath.'[33] He divides the works into two main categories. First, works that relate to Muslim influence upon the European literary tradition, particularly the English literary tradition. He cites here the influence of '*futuwwah*' works upon the formation of the 'Western tradition of chivalry' or 'the influence of *Alf Laylā wa Laylā* on the English literature.'[34] Second, are the works relating to the perception of Muslims and Islam in English literature. This is the more popular type with an 'abundance of dissertations, books, and research articles about various genres of literary writing covering several centuries of literary history.'[35] I shall provide a selection of works below that fall into the second category. This dissertation does not strictly fall into either of these categories.

My aim is not to demonstrate 'Attār's influence on *The Faerie Queene* and neither do I seek to construct an 'image' of the perceptions of Muslims or Islam in *The Faerie Queene*. My primary aim is to focus upon both texts

---

[33] Hafiz Abid Masood, 'Islam in Medieval and Early Modern English Literature: A Select Bibliography', *Islamic Studies*, 44 (2005), 553-629 (p. 554).
[34] Masood, *Islam*, p. 554.
[35] Masood, *Islam*, p. 554.

with the purpose of drawing on what they have to say about the Christian and Muslim believers journey to God. There are a number of works, cited below, that primarily deal with Islam and Muslim perceptions in *The Faerie Queene*. These explore the encounter with the Muslim *other*, through the prism of the crusades, political, social and economic power, but none to my knowledge that take the religious allegory of *The Faerie Queene* and compare it with an Islamic text, such as the *Conference of the Birds*, with the aim of extrapolating what we might learn from them regarding spiritual journeying. However, these works are useful in helping to shine a light on the political and historical allegory embedded within the text of *The Faerie Queene*, thereby demonstrating the multi-layered meanings inherent within the text.

Robinson has argued that central to the formation of English identity was the engagement with the Muslim *other*, the term 'Saracen' was applied liberally to draw into the net the whole of the Islamic world. Romance was the preeminent literary tool for the formation of European identities. He argues that Spenser, in *The Faerie Queene*, utilises the term 'Saracen' by transforming the romance use of it, in such a way that it becomes a simultaneous signifier, of 'both an encounter with Islam and the internal instability of Christendom.'[36] Robinson makes the point that in Protestant polemics 'Philip of Spain and his Armada' are popularised as the Souldan (*sultān*: Ottoman King) and by doing so, Spenser seeks to undermine Philip's claim to be fighting a holy war on behalf of Christendom, whereas for Spenser, the singleness of the Christian faith, points to the 'single Protestant nation.'[37] The conflation between the *Sultān* and Philip also feeds into the 'Protestant apocalyptic histories, which emphasized the identity of Islam and Catholicism as manifestations of Antichrist and forms of false belief.'[38] Conversely, the Catholic polemicists argued that Islam was an 'example of a claim to reform gone wrong' and they 'accused the Protestants of imitating Turks.'[39] Vitkus explores *Othello*, arguing that there was 'collective anxiety about religious conversion', leading to a fear of the enemy within, that is Catholics and the enemy without, the Ottomans, because of their conquering of Christian lands. As a consequence, both

---

[36] Benedict S. Robinson, *Islam and Early Modern Literature: The Politics of Romance from Spenser to Milton* (Palgrave Milton, 2007), [e-book], <http://0-www.myilibrary.com.catalogue.libraries.london.ac.uk?ID=173721> [accessed on 30 August 2016]. p. 33.

[37] Robinson, *Islam*, p. 42
[38] Robinson, *Islam*, p. 43.
[39] Robinson, *Islam*, p. 43.

were imagined as the representatives of the Anti-Christ and Satan, luring Protestant souls to damnation.[40] What is interesting about the anxiety about conversion, is that 'Attār uses this as a literary device to shock his Muslim audience, when he narrates the story of the conversion to Christianity and movement to Rome, of Sheikh Sam'ān, but at the same time makes this the basis for the transformation of the Sheikh's spiritual being.

Akbari argues that the negative depiction of Islam and the Prophet Muhammad is more a reflection of the inherent tensions within Christian societies in Europe. She suggests that the battle with Duessa in her headdress of 'Persian mitre' signifies the east, therefore, of Islam and the Saracen knights, who are 'faithless Sarazin' and his brother 'a proud Paynim' represent that evil enemy. Through these depictions, Spenser points to the apocalyptic nature of the struggle between good and evil.[41] Manion explores early modern literature through the prism of crusading narratives and aims to show 'enduring links between holy war and personal salvation.'[42] He focuses on literature from the late medieval to early modern period. For our purposes, he acknowledges that *The Faerie Queene* is a complex work and cannot be reduced to a political reading but is multi-layered with meanings. He considers the Redcrosse knight's cross and shield as a 'symbol of the English nation and as a crusader.'[43] It also symbolises the militaristic role of the knight, reflecting the 'injunctions of crusade sermons and discourse, which used biblical citations about taking up Jesus' cross and following him to explicate crusading.'[44]

Despite these extremely negative portrayals, there were glimmers of positive images too. Matar has argued that preachers and theologians, had constructed a distorted and negative image of Muslims and Islam. However, those who travelled to Muslim lands for business or as diplomats,

---

[40] Daniel J. Vitkus, 'Turning Turk in Othello: the conversion and damnation of the Moor', *Shakespeare Quarterly*, 48 (1997), 145-176 (p. 145).

[41] Suzanne Conklin Akbari, 'The rhetoric of antichrist in Western lives of Muhammad', *Islam and Christian-Muslim Relations*, 8 (1997), 297-307 (p. 303-304).

[42] Lee Manion, *Narrating the Crusades: Loss and Recovery in Medieval and Early Modern English Literature* (Cambridge: Cambridge University Press, 2014), p. 146. <http://dx.doi.org/10.1017/CBO9781107415218>

[43] *Manion, Narrating, p. 167.*

[44] *Manion, Narrating, p. 167.*

wrote stories that were humanising of the *other*.[45] Although both Robinson, et al., provide useful insights, I shall though argue, that Spenser's intention as stated in his letter to Raleigh was one about the spiritual and virtuous formation of Redcrosse knight and thereby every Christian man, rather than an anti-Catholic and anti-Islamic polemic. It is here that I believe there is common thread or ground between both Spenser's and Attār's works. For as Lewis has rightly argued, Spenser's aim was not to find differences but agreements. These entail syncretism of ideas that the modern sceptical mind finds distrustful. He argues that Spenser 'welded together, so many diverse elements, Protestant, chivalric, Platonic, Ovidian, Lucretian, and pastoral', that because of this we might 'feel that he must have been very vague and shallow in each.'[46] The modern mind is trained to view each as a distinct category and any form of syncretism is despised. However, argues Lewis, Spenser's assumptions are different from ours:

> [...] he assumed from the outset that the truth about the universe was knowable and in fact known. If that were so, then of course you would expect agreements between the great teachers of all ages just as you expect agreements between the reports of different explorers. The agreements are the important thing, the useful and interesting thing.[47]

Lewis, cites Professor Osgood as stating that this is what makes *The Faerie Queene*, 'somehow unmeasurable.' Spenser seeks to articulate to his readers 'not his philosophy but their own experience - everyone's experience – loosened from its particular contexts by the universalizing power of allegory.'[48] It is precisely this universal allegory that unites Attār and Spenser, and within which lies the appeal of the texts that transcends religious and cultural barriers. Most of the recent scholarly focus has been on the *othering* of Muslims and Islam in English literature, however, I envisage the two texts as bridges between Christian and Muslim faithful. This I believe to be a much more fruitful and personally, a rewarding enterprise.

---

[45] Nabil Matar, 'Britons and Muslims in the early modern period: from prejudice to (a theory of) toleration', *Patterns of Prejudice*, 43 (2009), 213-231.
[46] C. S. Lewis, *English Literature in the Sixteenth Century Excluding Drama* (Oxford: OUP, 1973). P. 386.

[47] Lewis, *English*, p. 387.
[48] Lewis, *English*, p. 387.

3 THE FAERIE QUEENE – BOOK ONE

Spenser's aim was to compile twenty-four books, the first twelve being dedicated to the twelve Aristotelian moral virtues, and second, set of twelve on 'public' virtues, alas he was only able to complete the first six books before his death. In each book, a knight goes on an adventure to achieve perfection of one of the virtues; by doing so, the reader is drawn into the world of the faerie land, constructed by Spenser, through which he discovers the nature, obstacles and challenges on the path to achieving that particular virtue.

A VISION OF GLORIANA

In his letter to Raleigh, Spenser points to the spiritual vision of Arthur and his quest to find the Faery Queene:

> to have seene in a dreame or vision the Faery Queen, with whose excellent beauty rauished, he awakening resolved to seeke her out [..] he went to seeke her forth in Faerye land. In that Faery Queene I meane glory in my generall intention, but in my particular I conceiue the most excellent and glorious person of our soueraine the Queene, and her kingdome in Faery land.[49]

This vision is the catalyst for Arthur's journey and clearly, is of such a nature that it is the spark that ignites his quest in search of Gloriana. The uniqueness of this vision of the Faery Queene lies in Arthur's soliloquy, canto 1.ix.14:

---

[49] Spenser, *Faerie Queene*, p. 716.

> Ne liuing man like words did euer heare,
> As she to me deliuered all that night;

This clearly entails a spiritual vision reflecting 1 Cor. 2.9 that those who love God will see in heaven - what no eye or ear has seen or heard. For our purposes, it also shows that the ultimate end of all-spiritual questing is Gloriana, not just for Arthur but for all his Christian readers. Lewis suggests that for the Christian, 'glory is what awaits the faithful in heaven' and that 'the sight of true Honour was the vision of God'.[50] He also argues that Arthur is moved by his vision of Gloriana not because he witnesses the earthly glory of a monarch but Divine Glory, the earthly representation being a shadow of the Heavenly One. But even if we consider the reference to Gloriana literally, to be Queen Elizabeth I, we must bear in mind that for Spenser and his audience, 'all reigning sovereigns were *ex officio* vicegerents and images of God'.[51]

At the outset of the poem, Spenser has pointed to the aim of his work being to realise God. Redcrosse knight therefore becomes the personification of every Christian person, on a journey to spiritual perfection with each major battle, each confrontation with a dangerous foe, embodying an enemy that one has to overcome to achieve spiritual glory at the end of the spiritual journey. As we move to explore Redcrosse knight, we must bear in mind, and a point that should become apparent, that this spiritual journeying 'is not a state in which there is no sin, for that has been impossible since the Fall: it is a state in which one sins and is forgiven, so that no fall need be final and the Christian can resume his quest after each lapse.'[52]

THE REDCROSSE KNIGHT

What is striking initially about Redcrosse knight is his ordinariness, he could be any person and that is what Spenser's aim is, that he be seen as everyman.[53] His description in the first instance gives this impression, 'there presented him selfe a tall clownishe younge man',[54] but immediately

---

[50] Lewis, *English Literature*, p. 382.

[51] Lewis, *English Literature*, p. 383.

[52] Evans, Maurice, *Spenser's Anatomy of Heroism: A Commentary on The Faerie Queene* (Cambridge: Cambridge University Press, 1970), p. 89.

[53] Michael Murrin, 'The Audience of The Faerie Queene', *Explorations in Renaissance Culture*, 23 (1997), 1-21. He argues that the chivalric romance was a form of fiction that appealed across the diverse classes of society.

the ordinariness is obliterated and replaced with a deep aspiration for a great task. He falls to the ground desiring a boon of some adventure from the Faerie Queene, whilst the Faerie Queene is in a state of reflection, a 'fair Ladye' enters the room bearing armour of a knight and petitions the Faerie Queene for help to release her parents, who are King and Queen imprisoned in a brazen castle. After reflection and insistence of the young man to be given the task at hand, his petition is granted and the Lady informs him that he must put on the armour, otherwise he will not succeed in the enterprise. As soon as he does, 'he seemed the goodliest man in al that company, and was well liked of the Lady.'[55]

As we proceed with our reading we discover that the faire Ladye symbolises Una, the Christian Truth, and that the King and Queene who have been imprisoned, represent Adam and Eve.[56] In the words of Frye:

> The quest of the Redcrosse knight in Book I follows the symbolism of the quest of Christ. He carries the same emblem of a red cross on a white ground; the monster he has to kill is "that old dragon" (quatrain to Canto xi; cf. Rev. xii, 9) who is identical with the Biblical Satan, Leviathan, and serpent of Eden, and the object of killing him is to restore Una's parents, who are Adam and Eve, to their kingdom of Eden, which includes the entire world, now usurped by the dragon.[57]

The clownish young man, an upstart, who seems to have no experience of combat or anything remarkable about him, is suddenly transformed through taking on the armour that the Lady has brought with her. In Canto I stanza 1, Redcrosse knight is described as bearing 'mightie armes and silver shielde' but in description of the shield Spenser states, 'Wherein old dints of deepe woundes did remaine / The cruell markes of many a bloody fielde; Yet armes till that time did he never wielde.' The armour Redcrosse knight has been given is well tried, battle hardened and is of a mighty nature but we are informed, he though, has never experienced any combat. His shield bears the red cross, which was the recognised symbol of St George and also as noted below in Ephesians, is 'the shield of

---

[54] Spenser, *Faerie Queene*, p. 717.

[55] Spenser, *Faerie Queene*, p. 717.

[56] A. C. Hamilton, 'Spenser's "Letter to Ralegh"', *Modern Language Notes*, 73 (1958), 481-485 (p. 484).

[57] Northrop Frye, 'The Structure of Imagery in The Faerie Queene', in *Essential Articles for the study of Edmund Spenser*, ed. by A. C. Hamilton (Connecticut: Archon Books, 1972), pp. 153-170 (p. 162).

faith.'

'ARMOUR OF GOD'

The question is how is it able to transform the clownish young man into someone worthy to take on a task of huge magnitude? Spenser in his letter to Raleigh points to his source of the armour being Ephesians 6.11-17. The obvious point to remember is that by deploying the armour and the shield as a free gift bestowed upon the Redcrosse knight, Spenser is alluding to what would be a common belief in the Elizabethan period articulated in Article XI of the Thirty-Nine Articles, 'we are accounted righteous before God only for the merit of our Lord and Saviour Jesus Christ by Faith, and not for our own works or deservings.'[58] However, this doesn't quite draw out the depth of meaning of the 'armour of God' that Redcrosse knight has been granted and that has been transformative.

Developing the themes of armour and clothing, Gless argues, that the metaphor of clothing plays a central role in the individual Christians journey to holiness. There is a sense here that the outward 'putting on Christ' is also the act of taking on a new psychic and spiritual disposition.[59] Henry Smith suggests that putting on Christ is to sum up the totality of Biblical teaching. Gless argues that both the metaphor of 'putting on' Christ and the armour, signify 'justification and sanctification, both gifts of Christ.' It signifies, in the words of St Paul, Christ 'doth cover us like a garment [...] [which] hideth our unrighteousness with his righteousness [...] that the wrath of God cannot find us.' The armour, on the other hand becomes a shield of protection, 'This garment is called an armor, because it defendeth us from all the assaults of the devil, the flesh, the world, the heat of persecution, and the cold of defection.'[60] This does not mean though, that the individual Christian will be immune from pain and suffering in the world, on the contrary, in the words of Perkins, 'the right way to go unto heaven, is to sail by hell, and there is no man living that feeleth the power and virtue of the blood of Christ, which first hath not felt the pains of hell.'[61]

The Redcrosse knight and the Christian person must imitate the death

---

[58] Virgil K. Whitaker, 'The Theological Structure of The Faerie Queene, Book I', in *Essential Articles for the study of Edmund Spenser*, ed. by A. C. Hamilton (Connecticut: Archon Books, 1972), pp. 101-112 (p. 104).
[59] Darryl J. Gless, *Interpretation and Theology in Spenser* (Cambridge: Cambridge University Press, 1994), p. 45.
[60] Gless, *Interpretation*, p. 45-46.
[61] Gless, *Interpretation*, p. 45.

and resurrection in his life, if he is to achieve his task. As St Paul says in Rom. 6:3-6, that the baptism in Christ signifies the baptism in his death, and therefore just as he 'was raised up from the dead by the glory of the Father, so we also should walk in newness of life [...] our old man is crucified with him, that the body of sin might be destroyed, that henceforth we should not serve sin.' Gless argues that this 'new life' is a state in which there is continuous 'inner deaths and resurrections, an alternation through which the believer can "put on the new man, which after God is created in righteousness, and true holiness (Eph. 4:24)"'.[62]

Gless suggests that the red cross emblazoned on the shield and breast of Redcrosse knight, points to his identity as a Christian warrior. This identity is 'sufficiently vague' so as to be open to a multiple set of doctrinal interpretations. He argues that the blood on the cross can act as an 'emblem of the Lord who died once in order to live and send aid to His knights for ever.' It can also point to the spiritual presence of Christ, that his blood now becomes 'as a physical reality (that actually shed at the crucifixion) which can now symbolize, for knight and reader, a real spiritual presence.'[63] The symbolism of the cross at the outset, Gless argues, signifies that 'to be holy is to "put on" Christ, to exist by grace "in Him."'[64]

Leslie notes that the symbolism of warfare became an early point of iconographical focus symbolising 'the struggle between good and evil' and that:

> The depiction of Christ with the attributes of a soldier is found as early as the Book of Revelations. From this beginning Christ the warrior, or Christ the victor, becomes one of the great traditional images of medieval art; and its popularity goes hand in hand with a progressive modulation into the forms and styles of chivalry.'[65]

This was further developed through commentaries, sermons, scriptural and allegorical readings of Is. 11:4-5; 59:16-18; Rev. 12:7, to denote the individual Christian as the soldier, in imitation of Christ, in battle with forces of evil and wickedness. Through use of the armour and the shield, Spenser is drawing on 'the device of the *miles Christi* throughout the ages,

---

[62] Gless, *Interpretation*, p. 45

[63] Gless, *Interpretation*, p. 52.

[64] Gless, *Interpretation*, p. 54.

[65] Michael Leslie, *Spenser's 'Fierce Warres and Faithfull Loves': Martial and Chivalric Symbolism in 'The Faerie Queene'* (Cambridge: D. S. Brewer, 1983), p. 101.

and of St George, the Crusaders, St Michael in the defeat of Satan, and Christ himself.'[66]

St Paul's use of the symbolism of the 'whole armour of God', Leslie argues, is to demonstrate its transformative nature. What Spenser is pointing to is the immediate transformation of the individual Christian through the act of taking on the new clothing (Rev. 6:3-6). In the words of Leslie:

> [...] the transformation of the individual from the Old Man of the pre-Christian era to the New Man of Christianity. This change, potential not automatic, requires an effort on the part of the individual to overcome his own propensities for evil. And it is in connection with the Christian's internal struggle that the martial metaphors are used.[67]

The full implications of the term 'whole armour of God' becomes fully apparent in the light of St Paul's theology. Citing Rom. 6.12-13, Leslie argues that 'St Paul associates the Christian's weapons with his body' and therefore 'the limbs of the body are seen as weapons, potentially employable for good or ill.'[68] He argues that the body is at the centre of St Paul's theological vision and that he sees it as journeying through three stages on its way to salvation. The first stage corresponds to sin and is before the coming of Christ, the second, is 'the Incarnation, when Christ assumed our flesh', this means Christians are not completely free of sin but are baptised in one body with Christ. The third stage, will be on the last judgement day, when Christians are perfected in Christ.[69]

These three stages are reflected in Redcrosse knight's battle with the dragon in canto 11. The first stage is his fall into the 'well of life',[70] which has the characteristic of:

> For vnto life the dead it could restore,
> And guilt of sinfull crimes cleane wash away,
> Those that with sicknesse were infected sore,
> It could recure, and aged long decay
> Renew, as one were borne that very day.[71]

---

[66] Leslie, *Spenser's*, p. 102.
[67] Leslie, *Spenser's*, p. 106.
[68] Leslie, *Spenser's*, p. 106.
[69] Leslie, *Spenser's*, p. 106-107.
[70] 1.xi.29.9

The immersion into the 'well of life' renews the sick from the illness of sin, this being equated to death, into a new life, 'so new this new-borne knight to battell new did rise.'[72] Leslie suggests that just as Redcrosse knight's armour has been renewed, likewise, his body too has gone through 'renewal, regeneration, and transformation.'[73] This reflects St Paul's teaching on the transformative nature of baptism, in the words of Robinson:

> The resurrection of the body starts at baptism, when a Christian becomes 'one Spirit' (i.e., one spiritual body) with the Lord (I Cor.6.17), and 'puts on (the body of) Christ' (Gal.3.27), 'the new man', which 'hath been created' (Eph.4.24) and 'is being renewed [...] after the image of him that created him' (Col.3.10).[74]

This baptismal regeneration also answers Kaske's objection that such armour cannot be the armour of the Christian man because rather than protect Redcrosse knight, it helps 'the flame to sear instead of singe his entire body instead of his face, so that he decides to take it off.'[75] Leslie's response to this criticism is insightful. He argues that Redcrosse knight's responses to the searing fire is two-fold. In the first instance (i.xi.26.6-9), the flame is of such intensity that the armour, rather than a source of protection, becomes the instrument of inflicting pain upon him, thereby leading him to remove it. However, in the second instance (1.xi.28.1-5), Leslie argues that it refers to Redcrosse knight's spiritual state in which 'death did he oft desire.' These are to be understood, not in their literal sense, but in the light of St Paul's teaching. That the removal of the armour 'represents a body which, infected with sin and death, has become intolerable.' This is what Spenser is pointing out when he states that the flame seared Redcrosse knight's entire body, that would include the armour.[76] To offer further weight to his argument, Leslie cites Rom. 7.24 pointing to the wretchedness of the body as an instrument of sin and death. He states:

---

[71] 1.xi.30.1-5.

[72] 1.xi.34.9.

[73] Leslie, *Spenser's*, p. 108.

[74] Leslie, *Spenser's*, p. 108.

[75] Carol V. Kaske, 'The Dragon's Spark and Sting and the Structure of Red Cross's Dragon-Fight: The Faerie Queene, I.xi-xii', in *Essential Articles for the study of Edmund Spenser*, ed. by A. C. Hamilton (Connecticut: Archon Books, 1972), pp. 425-446 (p. 433).

[76] Leslie, *Spenser's*, p. 110.

> St Paul wishes to be free of the body in its unredeemed state. The closeness of the Romans passage suggests that it is the body itself that the Red Cross Knight wishes to abandon, and that this is represented in his desire to remove his armour.[77]

What Spenser is suggesting here is that although human beings have been created in the image of God, nonetheless, the fall has led to a state in which the body is no longer an instrument of perfection but imperfection, thereby becoming an instrument of sin and death. That is the reason why the armour turns on Redcrosse knight as an instrument of torture because in the fallen state it is the 'chief weapon in the armoury of sin and death.'[78] Spenser wants to demonstrate the weakness of Redcrosse knight in the absence of baptism and his arrogance upon relying on his own strength. It is essential that a demarcation line is drawn between the pre-Christian man and the new-man, regenerated, transformed and ready for the battle but not yet fully transformed to strike a death knell to the dragon, the arch enemy of human kind.

In the second stage, the Redcrosse knight falls again but this time he is in control and no longer relies upon his strength but recognises the guidance of 'God for his safety.' This then points to the transformation that has taken place within the Redcrosse knight. Whereas, on the first day of battle, the Redcrosse knight's primary weapon is the spear, which is unable to withstand the fiery flame of the dragon, however, in the second day's battle, Spenser brings back into play the whole armour of Redcrosse knight. This is the 'shield of faith' quoted by St Paul in Ephesians (6.16) that 'above all, taking the shield of faith, wherewith ye shall be able to quench all the fiery darts of the wicked.'[79] In fact, Leslie suggests, the second day's battle is focused upon the shield and the dragon's struggle to wrestle it away from Redcrosse knight. It is through Redcrosse knight's fierce defence of his shield, that he is able to severely wound the dragon. Despite his heroic struggle, Redcrosse knight falls, though in a controlled way, below the *'tree of life.'* It is subsequent to this second transformation that he is ultimately victorious over the dragon. Leslie argues that the Redcrosse knight does not become Christ as suggested by Kaske, but in the light of 'St Paul's theology of the body, we may suggest that the Knight, as a result of Christ's death and resurrection, has become part of Christ the perfect man: not Christ, but "in Christ", to use St Paul's phrase.'[80]

---

[77] Leslie, *Spenser's*, p. 110.

[78] Leslie, *Spenser's*, p. 110.

[79] Leslie, *Spenser's*, p. 113.

[80] Leslie, *Spenser's*, p. 115.

Although Leslie's suggestion of a three stage process is useful, it nonetheless, misses a critical moment in Redcrosse knight's journey to his final victory. That stage, as I suggested in my introduction is his stay in the house of Holiness. Prior to this he almost commits suicide when he encounters Despair (Canto vii) and his captivity by Orgoglio (Canto viii) also demonstrates that he is lacking – not quite ready for the final encounter with the dragon. Broaddus has argued that the Redcrosse knight begins his career 'as one who is elect but unsaved' and is 'eventually called and justified in the house of Holiness.'[81] He suggests that Redcrosse knight's original desire for an adventure, to 'proue his puissance in battell brave'[82] and quoting Contemplation, he was, 'prickt with courage, and [...] [his] forces pryde,' 'to seeke for fame, / And proue[...] [his] puissant armes'[83] are in fact the obstacles in his journey to realise ultimate victory. These demonstrate that although they are desires that suit a romance form well, nonetheless, 'that desire provides one of the means by which Satan attempts to thwart God's plan for one of his elect.'[84] So the real issue for Redcrosse knight is his 'indiscriminate coveting of worldly fame' and therefore the necessity of Una bringing him to the house of Holiness.

HOUSE OF HOLINESS

Spenser describes the house as 'ancient', dedicated to the relief 'of wretched soules', and that 'all night she spent in bidding of her bedes, / And all the day in doing good and godly deeds.' One senses in this description immediately a movement from a stage, prior to this, of being self-centred to God-centred. At the core of the activity of this house is the saving and disciplining of souls. The head of the house, Dame Cælia, the 'heavenly one' introduces Redcrosse knight to her three daughters, *Fidelia* (faith), *Speranza* (hope), and *Charissa* (love). Una makes the request to *Fidelia*, 'To have her knight into her schoolehous plaste, / That of her heauenly learning he might taste, / And heare the wisedom of her words divine.'[85] She is a teacher and preacher with immense learning through understanding by faith. Bergvall makes a hugely insightful point that the key to understanding Book One is to understand Augustine's theory of signs and what *Fidelia* does is through the study of the words of the Christian Scripture lead Redcrosse knight to the 'transcendent Signifier,

---

[81] James W. Broaddus, 'Spenser's Redcrosse Knight and the Order of Salvation', *Studies in Philology*, 108 (2011), 572-604 (p. 573).

[82] 1.i.3

[83] 1.x.66

[84] Broaddus, *Spenser's Redcrosse*, p. 575.

[85] 1.x.18.4-6

which in turn provides for his deciphering other linguistic and existential signs.'[86]

Broaddus makes the point that Una, who stands for the Christian Truth, has been God's instrument that has guided, through her love for the knight, on a 'path to salvation' and that each time he departs from the path, she brings him back. In the words of Broaddus:

> Una's love for Redcrosse, a fusion of earthly and Christian love, also serves by contrast to illuminate the self-love that dominates the characterization of the Redcrosse Knight prior to his sojourn in the house of Holiness and contributes to the perception that he, although elect, begins his adventures possessed of a dead faith.[87]

His view challenges the position of Morgan, who has argued that Redcrosse knight's victory over Error was a result of his *adding faith* to his manly power. For Broaddus, it was Redcrosse knight's desire for worldly fame that enabled him victory over Error but his faith will attain 'spiritual victory only after he is justified, repents his sins, and begins the process of sanctification.'[88] The opening lines of canto x express, where the Redcrosse knight may have fallen short:

> What man is he, that boasts of fleshly might,
> And vaine assuraunce of mortality,
> Which all so soone, as it doth come to fight,
> Against spirituall foes, yields by and by,
> Or from the fielde most cowardly doth fly?
> Ne let the man ascribe it to his skill,
> That thorough grace hath gained victory.
> If any strength we haue, it is to ill,
> But all the good is Gods, both power and eke will.

His reliance has been heavily on his manly strength and that is no weapon against his spiritual foe, the dragon. What is interesting here is that Spenser is alluding to the weaponry required in this battle as being spiritual and not just manly strength. This could also be interpreted as the foe not being outward alone but inward within the spiritual or lack of, constitution of the Redcrosse knight. That then is the reason why Una finally brings

---

[86] Åke Bergvall, 'The Theology of the Sign: St Augustine and Spenser's Legend of Holiness', *Studies in English Literature*, 33 (1993), 21-42 (p. 35).
[87] Broaddus, *Spenser's Redcrosse*, p. 579.
[88] Broaddus, *Spenser's Redcrosse*, p. 580.

him to the house of Holiness.

Padelford argues that *Fidelia's* core teaching articulate Calvinistic doctrine, '*Fidelia* opens her book, that none untaught could read, and teaches of God, of grace, of jutice, and of free-will-the very core of Calvinistic doctrine'[89] and that Redcrosse knight achieves faith and thereby consciousness of sin through *Fidelia*. Broaddus disagrees with Padelford's contention that Redcrosse knight has gained faith through *Fidelia's* instruction. He argues that Calvin taught that man could not know God without first having been recipient of grace, 'Now, no man is truly persuaded that he is of God, except he has previously received his grace.'[90] Broaddus takes the view that after Redcrosse knight 'hearing the Gospel, preached by *Fidelia*, God extends the inward calling through the power of the Holy Spirit, and Redcrosse is received into a state of grace, into "the perfection of all heauenly grace."'[91] But in addition to this, Calvin argues for the essential role of the Holy Spirit:

> This simple and external demonstration of the Divine word ought, indeed, to be fully sufficient for the production of faith, if it were not obstructed by our blindness and perverseness. But such is our propensity to error, that our mind can never adhere to Divine truth; such is our dullness, that we can never discern the light of it. Therefore nothing is effected by the word, without the illumination of the Holy Spirit [...] Therefore, as we can never come to Christ, unless we are drawn by the Spirit of God, so when we are drawn, we are raised both in mind and in heart above the reach of our own understanding.[92]

A transformation begins to take place in the Redcrosse knight, there now seems to be theological understanding accompanied with genuine remorse in his previous sinfulness and the full comprehension of the implications of his 'wicked ways.' Redcrosse knight's state is beautifully expressed by Spenser:

> The faithfull knight now grew in little space,
> By hearing her, and by her sisters lore,
> To such perfection of all heauenly grace;
> That wretched world he gan for to abhore

---

[89] Broaddus, *Spenser's Redcrosse*, p. 586.
[90] Broaddus, *Spenser's Redcrosse*, p. 587.
[91] Broaddus, *Spenser's Redcrosse*, p. 587.
[92] Broaddus, *Spenser's Redcrosse*, p. 587-588.

> And mortall life gan loath, as thing forlore,
> Greeud with remembrance of his wicked wayes,
> And prickt with anguish of his sinnes so sore
> That he desirde, to end his wretched days:
> So much the dart of sinfull guilt the soule dismayes.[93]

Broaddus suggests that the key word here is 'grew' and represents Redcrosse knight's inward transformation. This has not only been a result of her sisters tutelage but through the workings of the Holy Spirit, Redcrosse knight has been brought 'justification, the imputation of righteousness' and 'the beginning of repentance.'[94] Redcrosse knight expresses the thought of taking his life, 'That he desirde, to end his wretched days' because of his comprehension of the gravity of his sinfulness. Some have interpreted this to be a sign of his repentance, others however, understand this as Redcrosse knight's return to the psychological torment in his encounter with Despair:

> William Nelson says that when Redcrosse "listens to the teaching of Fidelia in the house of Holiness he is driven [by frustration] to a despairing wish for death." A. Leigh DeNeef says, "Fidelia's instruction, which begins as the attempt to correct Despair's false teaching, leads to the same anguished result." David Lee Miller says that the "reading lesson enters into the pattern of blindness-and-vision we encounter on the Mount of Contemplation, and inevitably produces its own moment of revulsion."[95]

Broaddus responds by arguing that the comparison with Redcrosse knight's encounter with Despair is to miss the point, he now has faith and attained Christ. When Calvin spoke of 'desiring death' he meant this to be understood in the light of human iniquity, drawing a distinction with those might desire death because of the weariness of life. In the case of the Redcrosse knight, Calvin's following words are more apt, 'But it must be added, that though the faithful level at the mark, they are not carried away by an unbridled desire in wishing for death, but submit themselves to the will of God, to whom it behoves us both to live and die.'[96]

---

[93] 1.x.21

[94] Broaddus, *Spenser's Redcrosse*, p. 588.

[95] Broaddus, *Spenser's Redcrosse*, p. 589.

[96] Broaddus, *Spenser's Redcrosse*, p. 590.

4 CONFERENCE OF THE BIRDS

The *Conference of the Birds* is one of the most sublime allegorical works in the Persian language. It is a work rooted in Sūfism, the spiritual heart of the Islamic tradition and describes the Sūfī's journey to God.[97] It is also a commentary on a famous *hadīth* (tradition) of the Prophet, 'Whoso knoweth himself knoweth his Lord.'[98] Birds of the world, representing various seekers of the spiritual way to God, are brought together to seek out their King – the Sīmorgh. Initially the birds are excited but when the arduous nature of the journey dawns on them, they begin to proffer various excuses on why they cannot join the spiritual quest. These excuses represent voices of various human beings, and the excuses they might provide against journeying to God. Morris has expressed the influence and significance of this work in the following words:

> Conference of the Birds is not just a literary masterpiece: its wider popular influence throughout the Eastern Islamic world, both directly and through centuries of retelling of its stories by subsequent writers in Persian, Turkish, Urdu, and other vernacular languages, can only be compared, for example, to the place of Milton, Bunyan, or even the King James Bible in pre-twentieth-

---

[97] 'Attār, *Conference*, p. 14.
[98] Muhyiddīn Ibn al-'Arabī, *Whoso Knoweth Himself...*, tran. by The Muhyiddīn Ibn 'Arabī Society (Abingdon: Beshara Publications, 1988). This is an excellent commentary on this Prophetic tradition explaining with great precision and profundity, as well clarifying the erroneous view noted by Darbandi and Davis, the translators of the *Conference of the Birds*, that Shaykh Ibn al-'Arabī is a pantheist.

century Anglo-Saxon culture. 'Attār's primary aim, in this and all his other writings was to bring the spiritual teachings and insights of the Qur'ān and hadīth (the sayings of the Prophet Muhammad), as they had been understood by earlier generations of saints and Sufis...'[99]

On their journey to discover the Sīmorgh, the birds must traverse the seven valleys – these are the valleys of the Quest, Love, Gnosis, Detachment, Unity of God, Bewilderment, Poverty and Nothingness - each signifying an essential aspect of the journey of personal self-discovery. When they eventually enter into the presence of the Sīmorgh, instead of seeing Him, they all see their own reflections:

> There in the Simorgh's radiant face they saw
> Themselves, the Simorgh of the world – with awe
> They gazed, and dared at last to comprehend
> They were the Sīmorgh and the journey's end.

'Attār here is playing on the pun *Sī* (thirty) *Morgh* (birds), that is the number of birds who eventually reach the end of their journey. In the words of Schimmel, 'this is the most ingenious pun in Persian literature, expressing so marvelously the experience of the identity of the soul with the divine essence.'[100]. Zwanzig suggests that for 'Attār the individual only sees his or her own reflection 'because the true image of God is too great for the mind to comprehend. Thus, the understanding and realisation of this leads the individual to dissolution, *fana.*'[101] In his masterful exposition of Sūfism, al-Hujwīrī explains the states of *fanā'* (annihilation in God) and *baqā'* (subsistence in God) in the following words:

> that annihilation comes to a man through vision of the majesty of God and through the revelation of Divine omnipotence to his

---

[99] James Winston Morris, 'Reading the Conference of the Birds', in *Approaches to the Asian Classics*, ed. by William Theodore De Bary and Irene Bloom (New York: Columbia University Press, 1990), pp. 77-85 (p. 77).
[100] Schimmel, *Mystical*, p. 307.
[101] Rebekah Zwanzig, 'Why must God Show himself in Disguise? An Exploration of Sufism within Farid Attar's "The Conference of the Birds"', in *Studies on Themes and Motifs in Literature: Disguise, Deception, Trompe-L'oeil: Interdisciplinary Perspectives*, ed. by Leslie Boldt, Corrado Federici and Virgulti Ernesto (New York: Peter Lang, 2008). pp. 273-284 (p. 284). ProQuest. [*online*].

heart, so that in the overwhelming sense of His majesty this world and the next world are obliterated from his mind, and "states" and "stations" appear contemptible in the sight of his aspiring thought, and what is shown to him of miraculous grace vanishes into nothing: he becomes dead to reason and passion alike, dead even to annihilation itself; and in that annihilation of annihilation his tongue proclaims God, and his mind and body are humble and abased, as in the beginning when Adam's posterity were drawn forth from his loins without admixture of evil and took the pledge of servantship to God (Kor. Vii, 171).[102]

So having been stripped of the Self, the birds are annihilated in the Sīmorgh:

Then, as they listened to the Sīmorgh's words,
A trembling dissolution filled the birds –
The substance of their being was undone,
And they were lost like shade before the sun;
Neither the pilgrims nor their guide remained.
The Sīmorgh ceased to speak, and silence reigned.[103]

Following this state of annihilation and subsistence, they are restored to their selves again, signifying the end of the journey for the Sūfī master, who can now be a true guide for others. 'Attār reminds the reader that the knowledge of their experience is a secret never to be divulged and will always contain an error when it is articulated because it relates to spiritual experience:

And then those birds, who were content to die,
To vanish in annihilation, saw

---

[102] 'Alī b. 'Uthmān al-Jullābī al-Hujwīrī, *Kashf al-Mahjūb: The Revelation of the Veiled*, trans. by Reynold A. Nicholson (Warminster: E. J. W. Gibb Memorial Trust, 2000), p. 246. See also, Andrew Wilcox, 'The Dual Mystical Concepts of *Fanā'* and *Baqā* in Early Sūfism', *British Journal of Middle Eastern Studies*, 38 (2011), 95-118. Wilcox provides a study of these Sūfī technical terms in the light of the teachings of the two major representatives of the schools of Baghdād and Khurāsān – Abū'l-Qāsim al-Junayd (d. 910) and Husayn ibn Mansūr al-Hallāj (d. 922). He has argued for four main mystical connotations of *fanā'* and *baqā'* (p. 116).
[103] 'Attār, *Conference*, p. 220.

> Their Selves had been restored to them once more,
> That after Nothingness they had attained
> Eternal life, and self-hood was regained.
> This Nothingness, this Life, are states no tongue
> At any time has adequately sung.[104]

In the following sections I will begin with 'Attār's description and symbolism of the Sīmorgh, and then focus on the story of Shaykh Sam'ān.

A VISION OF SĪMORGH

> It was in China, late one moonless night,
> The Sīmorgh first appeared to mortal sight –
> He let a feather float down through the air,
> And rumours of its fame spread everywhere;
> Throughout the world men separately conceived
> An image of its shape, and all believed.[105]

Whereas Spenser in his letter to Raleigh outlines the vision of Prince Arthur of Gloriana, who we noted symbolised God. 'Attār similarly employs the character of the Sīmorgh to symbolise the King of the birds and introduces the Sīmorgh in the most exquisite introductory verses. In his description of the Sīmorgh, he alludes to his majesty, glory, uniqueness, power, immanence and transcendence. Space does not allow for a full treatment of the various allusions but by way of an example, I'll provide an explanation of the following lines 'And He is always near to us, though we / Live far from His transcendent majesty.'[106] These lines allude to the following two verses of the Qur'ān that captivated the Sūfī imagination:

> And when My servants question thee concerning Me, then surely I am nigh. I answer the prayer of the supplicant when he crieth unto Me. So let them hear My call and let them trust in Me, in order that they may be led aright. [2:186][107]

We verily created man and We know what his soul whispereth to

---

[104] 'Attār, *Conference*, p. 220-221.

[105] 'Attār, *Conference*, p. 34-35.

[106] 'Attār, *Conference*, p. 33.

[107] All Qur'ānic quotations are from Marmaduke Pickthall's translation found at www.altafsir.com unless otherwise stated.

him, and We are nearer to him than his jugular vein. [50:16]

These verses emphasise love, the immanence of God and the intimacy between God and His servants. In his commentary on 2:186, al-Razzāq interprets 'My servants' as pointing to the 'wayfarers, the seekers, those oriented towards Me', so in general those who are on a journey to God.[108] Maybudī elucidates this further citing the story of Moses when God spoke with him. Moses was overwhelmed by Divine love upon the experience of hearing the speech of God, he asked where should I seek You? The reply was:

> O Moses, seek as you like, for I am with you. I am nearer to you than the spirit in your body, your life-vein to you, your speaking to your mouth. The speech is My speech, the light is my light, and I am the Lord of the Worlds.[109]

On the love and intimacy God shows for his servant, Maybudī elucidating, *surely I am nigh. I answer the prayer of the suppliant when he crieth unto Me*, understands this as God is saying:

> I am near to My servants, and I love the near ones. I answer those who call to Me, I give access to those who seek Me, I am pleased with those who reach proximity to me. My servant! Come near to Me so that I may come near to you.[110]

The other significant point that 'Attār highlights is the relationship between the Sīmorgh and the birds/creation. Zwanzig suggests that his description reflects two metaphors to describe this relationship – shadow and shade. On the shadow, 'Attār states:

> When long ago the Sīmorgh first appeared –
> His face like the sunlight when the clouds have cleared –
> He cast unnumbered shadows on the earth,
> On each one fixed his eyes, and each gave birth.
> Thus we were born; the birds of every land
> Are still his shadows – think, and understand.
> If you had known this secret you would see

---

[108] 'Abd al-Razzāq, *Tafsīr al-Kāshānī*, trans. by Feras Hamza (Amman: RABIIT, no date of publication), p. 85.
[109] Rashīd al-Dīn Maybudī, *The Unveiling of the Mysteries and the Provision of the Pious*, trans. by William C. Chittick (Amman: RABIIT, 2014), p. 111-112.
[110] Maybudī, *The Unveiling*, p. 112.

The link between yourselves and Majesty.[111]

The metaphor of the birds being a 'shadow' of the Sīmorgh illustrates the intrinsic relationship between the two, signifying a relationship of the bird's dependence, as well as potentiality of nearness. Zwanzig cites Ibn al-'Arabī stating, 'Each thing in the Dust received from His Light in accordance with its own preparedness (*isti'dād*) and potentiality, just as the corners of a room receive light of a lamp and, due to the degree of their proximity to that light, increase in brightness and reception (*qabūl*)'. This means that the birds (humans) have the capacity to reflect this light in the most perfect way and that 'hold an important place within creation.'[112] The second metaphor of shade denotes that:

> The multitude of forms that masquerade
> Throughout the world spring from the Sīmorgh's shade.
> If you catch sight of His magnificence
> It is His shadow that beguiles your glance;
> The Sīmorgh's shadow and Himself are one;
> Seek them together, twinned in unison.[113]

This describes the inseparable relationship between the Sīmorgh and all the other forms in creation. The splendour and beauty we witness are but shadows and shade, emanating from the Sīmorgh, not the *being* itself.

By way of a cautionary note, not all Muslims accepted the intimate and personal relationship that 'Attār is a proponent of. The persecution of Sūfīs seems to have been particularly intense towards the end of the ninth century, when a Ghulām Khalīl, 'initiated an inquisition against the Baghdād Sūfīs.' Some 75 were 'summoned by authorities for interrogation' and their main crime seems to have been the advocacy of 'passionate love (*'ishq*) between humans and God. For Khalil, those who spoke of such impious matters were indistinguishable from adulterers.'[114]

---

[111] 'Attār, *Conference*, p. 52.

[112] Zwanzig, p. 277.

[113] 'Attār, *Conference*, p. 54.

[114] Atif Khalil, 'Abū Tālib al-Makkī & the Nourishment of Hearts (*Qūt al-qulūb*) in the Context of Early Sufism', *The Muslim World*, 102 (2012), 335-356 (p. 339). Khalil has provided a very good summary of Sūfīs responses to their opponents based upon the Qur'ān and *ahadīth*.

I will next explore the significance of the Sheikh Sam'ān story.

SHEIKH SAM'ĀN[115]

'Attār's two major themes of his poetry are 'the necessity for destroying the Self, and the importance of passionate love.'[116] In this powerful short story about Sheikh Sam'ān, 'Attār is able to provide an intense focus on both. The Sheikh is no ordinary Sūfī but one who has achieved great renown throughout the land, a symbol of asceticism through his intense fasting and prayer, he has performed fifty pilgrimages, worked miracles and 'was their living symbol of Belief.' One gets the sense of a man who has achieved great spiritual standing, however:

> A strange dream troubled him, night after night;
> Mecca was left behind; he lived in Rome,
> The temple where he worshipped was his home,
> And to an idol he bowed down his head.[117]

The Sheikh leaves for Rome with his four hundred disciples and is captivated, on arrival, by the beauty of a Christian girl:

> Love sacked his heart; the girl's bewitching hair
> Twined round his faith impiety's smooth snare.
> The sheikh exchanged religion's wealth for shame,
> A hopeless heart submitted to love's fame.[118]

The intensity of his love for the Christian girl is such that he converts to Christianity, drinks wine and becomes a swineherd. Yaghoobi provides an insightful analysis of what is happening here. She suggests, quoting Foucault, that the, 'subversion narrated' is a transgression of the 'limit' that 'opens violently onto the limitless, finds itself suddenly carried away by the content it had rejected and [is] fulfilled by this alien plenitude which invades it to the core of its being.'[119]

---

[115] In some manuscripts, the name is spelt San'ān but I have followed the translation of Afkham and Davies in which they use Sam'ān.

[116] 'Attār, *Conference*, p. 19.

[117] 'Attār, *Conference*, p. 58.

[118] 'Attār, *Conference*, p. 59.

[119] Claudia Yaghoobi, 'Subjectivity in 'Attār's Shaykh of San'ān Story in The Conference of the Birds', *CLCWeb: Comparative Literature and Culture*, 16.1 (2014), 1-10 (p. 6). <http://dx.doi.org/10.7771/1481-4374.2425>

This means that because the Sheikh has not 'experienced love and conformed to formalist Islam, by crossing the limit faces the alien content that he rejected previously and is carried away to the core of his being.' Although Sam'ān had initially sought to resist the demands of the Christian girl, he capitulated, thereby opening the limit to 'all its contents which he rejected so far.' This encounter with the other, is the moment through which 'Attar 'de- and reconstructs San'ān's identity' and significantly, this leads to the 'process of making and unmaking of his being.' Yaghoobi cites the work of Julia Kristeva, on the 'reconstruction of identity through love', Kristeva states:

> Love is the time and space in which "I" assumes the right to be extraordinary. Sovereign yet not individual. Divisible, lost, annihilated; but also, and through imaginary fusion with the loved one, equal to the infinite space of super-human psychism. Paranoid? I am, in love, at the zenith of subjectivity.[120]

Yaghoobi argues that although the Sheikh's 'crossing of the religious boundaries' is the highest transgression of Islamic law, it serves at the same time, as his surrendering 'to the will of god.' Citing Kristeva again, she argues that although the act of transgression makes both an unlikely couple, it though 'creates intimacy.' The Sheikh's love is directed to a higher object which is 'unattainable' but conversely the Sheikh also becomes the vehicle through which the Christian girl's love too is directed to this higher object. In the words of Yaghoobi:

> San'ān aspires to direct his love to a higher object and to an unattainable one. Not only does he aim for the unattainable, he guides his beloved towards the unattainable. But desiring the unattainable requires transcendence of the earthly and thus to reach the sublime, he needs to surpass his ego which has imprisoned him with worldly concerns and urges (Ritter 398). Only after he breaks the chains of his slavery to the self and crosses the lines of pretentious asceticism, does San'ān realize that the most important element on the path to the divine is love.[121]

This takes us to the second important theme of the Sheikh Sam'ān story and that is how does one break the 'chains of his slavery to the self?' Before I address this question, I think it would be useful to provide an alternative interpretation to the Sheikh Sam'ān narrative. What I have cited

---

[120] Yaghoobi, *Subjectivity*, p. 6.
[121] Yaghoobi, *Subjectivity*, p. 6.

above is one interpretation but for the purposes of exploring the 'self', I take the view that Mecca and the Ka'bah (Holy House) represent the human state before the descent to the earthly plane and that 'Rome' symbolises the world (*dunyā*). When at the end Sam'ān is returning home with his disciples, 'home' is not the earthly home but the realisation in his reconstructed identity of the primordial covenant (*mīthāq*). As has been noted by Henri Corbin, 'the religious conscience of Islām is centered upon a fact of meta-history.' On the same theme, Junayd states, 'This implies that in his final stage the worshipper returns to his first state, that he is as he was before he existed.'[122] What is this meta-history or state?

The *mīthāq* refers to the primordial covenant, mentioned in the Qur'ān 7:172, when God gathered all humanity in its spiritual forms and asked, 'Am I not your Lord?' and all replied, 'Yes, we witness it.' In the words of Schimmel:

> The idea of this primordial covenant (*mīthāq*) between God and humanity has impressed the religious conscience of the Muslims, and especially the Muslim mystics, more than any other idea. Here is the starting point for their understanding of free will and predestination, of election and acceptance, of God's eternal power and man's loving response and promise. The goal of the mystic is to return to the experience of the 'Day of *Alastu*', when only God existed…'[123]

THE GREATER JIHĀD

'Attār reminds the birds again and again, that the hindrance to their self-realisation is the Self. The Qur'ān refers to three characteristics of the Self or in Arabic '*nafs (pl. nufūs)*'. Winter suggests that these 'are not thought of as distinct stages, but rather as different aspects or potentials within the soul, which are all present simultaneously, some being latent and others active.'[124] The first is referred to as the *an-nafs al-ammāra bi's-su'* (the soul commanding to evil):

---

[122] Ali Hassan Abdel-Kader, *The Life, Personality and Writings of Al-Junayd*, (London: Luzac & Company Ltd, 1976), p. 76.

[123] Schimmel, *Mystical*, p. 24.

[124] Al-Ghazālī, *On Disciplining the Soul and Breaking the Two Desires: Books XXII and XXIII of The Revival of the Religious Sciences*, trans. by T. J. Winter (Cambridge: Islamic Texts Society, 2001), p. xxix.

> I do not exculpate myself. Lo! the (human) soul enjoineth unto evil, save that whereon my Lord hath mercy. Lo! my Lord is Forgiving, Merciful. [Q. 12:53]

This is the lower self in the 'biblical sense as "the flesh"'. It is this that the Prophet was referring to, when he said to his companions, 'we are coming from the lesser Jihād to the greater Jihād', to which the companions perplexed, responded that they thought fighting was the greater Jihād.[125] Al-Tirmidhī has argued that there are two types of Jihād. First, is fighting the enemy with the sword and the reward for this from God, is paradise. Second, is 'fighting passion and the self with the sword of renouncing one's will', and the reward for this is God's 'Throne' and 'proximity'[126] to Him.

In this state the human being becomes a slave to carnal desires (*hawā*) and is in utter disobedience to the dictates of Islamic teachings. In this state the *nafs* makes, 'such actions acceptable and appealing to the human being. Thus the *nafs* is described as enticing (*sawwalat*) subjecting (*tawwa'at*) and tempting (*tuwaswisu*) in Q. 20:96).' Picken suggests that the Arabic term *ammāra* has a sense of the *nafs*, 'constantly urging, always demanding, inciting and instigating' one towards evil.[127] He also notes that the description that the Qur'ān provides for the *nafs ammāra*, also applies to the characteristics of Satan. He quotes, al-Jawziyya:

> As for the soul inclined to evil (*al-nafs al-ammāra bi'l-sū*), Satan is its associate and companion; he makes promises to it and awakens its desires, casting falsehood into it, commanding it to evil and making it appear appealing in a form that it will find acceptable and condone, with a variety of provisions and falsehood, false hopes and destructive appetites. He seeks aid against it with its desires and wishes and through him every evil enters it.[128]

This is beautifully amplified by 'Attar when he speaks of the Sheikh captivated by the physical beauty of the Christian girl. But moreover, the idols, the drinking of wine and swine herding are not just outward but, 'This reverend sheikh kept swine – but who does not / Keep something swinish in his nature's plot?'[129] These are the 'idol-maker and idol-worshipper' that

---

[125] Schimmel, *Mystical*, p. 112.

[126] Al-Ghazālī, *Disciplining*, p. lxiii.

[127] Gavin Picken, 'Tazkiyat al-nafs: The Qur'anic Paradigm', *Journal of Qur'anic Studies*, 7 (2005), 101-127 (p. 112).

[128] Picken, *Tazkiyat*, p. 113.

is pointed to in verse 45:23, 'Hast thou seen him who maketh his desire his god'. That one's worldly desires alone become the single focus of one's existence leading to the forgetfulness of God. What 'Attār is arguing for here is that one can mock the Sheikh for his highest transgressions of the Islamic religious law but at least his love is sincere, even though misdirected. What is worse to worship idols outwardly or inwardly?

The second aspect of the *nafs* is *lawwāma* (self-reproaching). Picken notes that at this stage the 'veil of disobedience is lifted', the *nafs* begins to reproach itself for the evil that it has done and moves 'towards repentance, regret, self-recrimination and reproach.'[130] He further notes that there is a difference of opinion as to what this means and there are a number of interpretations. First, that the *nafs* is 'shifting repeatedly' from one to another and is 'characterised by its changeability, fickleness, capriciousness and inconsistency, never truly remaining steadfast upon one state of affairs.'[131] Second, that the *nafs* blames itself for the evil it has committed or feels blameworthiness for its disobedience. In the words of Jurjānī, 'It is the one [*al-nafs*] that is illuminated with the light of the heart according to the amount that it has become awakened from habitual heedlessness; as soon as it commits a transgression due to its naturally oppressive disposition it takes to blaming itself.'[132]

The aspect of the *nafs al-lawwāma* is exemplified in 'Attār's discourse between the disciple and the Sheikh. This, in the light of the description and characteristics of both the *ammāra* and *lawwāma*, becomes the dialogue between these two aspects of the Self. At this level 'Attār is articulating the dangers of passionate carnal desire:

> Another said: 'A demon's poisoned dart –
> Unknown to you – has pierced your trusting heart.'
> The shaikh said: 'If a demon straight from hell
> Deceives me, I rejoice and wish her well.'
> One said: 'Our noble sheikh has lost his way;
> Passion has led his wandering wits astray.'
> [...]
> Their words could not recall him to belief,
> And slowly they grew silent, sunk in grief.
> They watched; each felt the heart within him fail,

---

[129] 'Attār, *Conference*, p. 68.
[130] Picken, *Tazkiyat*, p. 113.
[131] Picken, *Tazkiyat*, p. 113.
[132] Picken, *Tazkiyat*, p. 114.

Fearful of deeds Fate hid beneath her veil.[133]

The third condition of the *nafs* is the *nafs* at peace and tranquility. The Qur'ān (89:27-30) states: *'But ah! thou soul at peace! (al-nafsu'l-mutma'innatu) Return unto thy Lord, content in His good pleasure! Enter thou among My bondmen! Enter thou My Garden!'* The battle with the *nafs* inciting evil and the cardinal pleasures has been won and the *nafs* is now reformed into a state of tranquility, calmness, serenity and peace: 'I will be brief; the sheikh was purified / According to the faith; his old self died.'[134] Picken notes that this state comes about, first, through the 'constant remembrance of God', he quotes Q. 13:28, *'Those who have believed and whose hearts become tranquil through the remembrance of God; isn't it through the remembrance of God that the hearts become tranquil?*' 'Attār writes, 'They prayed a hundred thousand prayers – at times' and also 'They neither ate nor slept but kept their gaze / Unswerving throughout forty nights and days.'[135] Mujāhid has defined this remembrance of God as 'that which cannot be forgotten under any circumstances' and at Qur'ān 58:19, those who forget God are compared to having become followers of Satan.[136]

Winter notes that the four key practices of self-discipline for early Sūfīs were 'solitude, silence, hunger and sleeplessness.'[137] When 'Attār speaks of the 'forty nights and days' he is referring to the spiritual seclusion, the purpose of which was to cut oneself off from the world and focus upon the remembrance of God. This was a common practice of the Prophet and the last ten days of Ramaḍān are often used for seclusion in the local mosque. The forty days and nights denotes a specific number for the seclusion. Tustarī suggests that whoever maintains a seclusion of forty days 'in true faith and sincerity, will have charismatic gifts (*karāmāt*) manifested to him from God.'[138] Silence was also emphasised, as the tongue was seen as the device for the vices of slander, backbiting, lying and cursing. Hunger was recognised as an important part of the seclusion, as it was considered to rein in the carnal desires of the flesh. Sleeplessness was considered to aid

---

[133] 'Attār, *Conference*, p. 62.

[134] 'Attār, *Conference*, p. 73.

[135] 'Attār, *Conference*, p. 71.

[136] Mir Valiuddin, *Contemplative Disciplines in Sufism*, ed. by Gulshan Khakee (London: East-West Publication, 1980), p. 32-33.

[137] Al-Ghazālī, *Disciplining*, p. xxix.

[138] Sahl b. 'Abd Allāh al-Tustarī, *Tafsīr al-Tustarī*, trans. by Annabel Keeler and Ali Keeler (Louisville: Fons Vitae, 2011), p. xx.

the seeker in utilising time effectively. Al-Ghazālī was of the view that 'sleep hardens and deadens the heart, unless, that is, one sleeps only in that amount which is needful, when it will conduce to the unveiling of the secrets of the Unseen.' Winter cites the story of Shāh al-Kirmānī who:

> [..] for forty years he never slept; then he fell asleep and dreamed of God. "O Lord!" he cried, "I was seeking Thee in nightly vigils, but I have found Thee in sleep". God answered: "O Shāh, you have found Me by means of those nightly vigils: if you had not sought Me there, you would not have found Me here".[139]

Picken also notes that the remembrance of God is strengthened through the second condition of *ridā'*, which has a 'very broad sense of satisfaction and acceptance of the religion of Islam', as mentioned by the Prophet, when he stated, 'The one who is contented with God as his Lord, Islam as his religion and Muhammad as his Prophet has truly "tasted the flavour of faith"'. Third, he suggests is particularly related to the sixth pillar of Islam that is faith in 'divine predestination (*al-qadā' wa'l-qadar*)'. He notes that it is possibly the most difficult to 'actualise' because 'it requires firm conviction (*yaqīn*) in God's overall wisdom and plan.' Fundamentally the reason for its perfection is its unquestioning submission to God 'no matter what befalls it in terms of human or personal tragedy.'[140] Jurjāni states:

> It is the one [al-nafs] whose illumination with the light of the heart has been completed to the extent that it has been divested of every blameworthy attribute and has been adorned with every praiseworthy characteristic.[141]

Qushayrī notes forty-three conditions that an aspirant must traverse to attain to the stage of peace and serenity. In addition, to what has been noted above, there is one that is absent in the analysis thus far but plays a central role; that is repentance, 'He kindles a repentant spark, the flame / Burns all our sins and all sin's burning shame.'[142] Al-Qushayri suggests that the first step on the journey to God is repentance (*tawba*). The term has a sense of 'return' or 'to come back', and means 'to return from what is blameworthy in the divine law to what is praiseworthy in it.'[143] The Prophet

---

[139] Al-Ghazālī, *Disciplining*, p. xxxii.
[140] Picken, *Tazkiyat*, p. 116.
[141] Picken, *Tazkiyat*, p. 116.
[142] 'Attār, *Conference*, p. 73.
[143] Abu'l-Qasim al-Qushayri, *Sufi Book of Spiritual Ascent: Al-Risala Al-*

said, 'regret is an act of repentance.' The person no longer remains in a state of heedlessness but has awoken acknowledging his sinfulness and disobedience, in the hope of forgiveness, 'The sea of righteousness drowns in its waves / The sins of those sincere repentance saves.'[144] The following holy tradition states well, the point that 'Attār is making regarding the worth of sincere repentance and also of hope in God:

> O child of Adam, as long as you beseech Me and hope for Me, I shall forgive you whatever you have done, without minding in the slightest. O child of Adam, were your sins to reach up to the clouds of Heaven and then you asked forgiveness of Me, I should forgive you, without minding in the slightest. O child of Adam, even if you were to bring Me enough sins to fill the earth, but then you met Me without associating anything with Me, I should bring to you the selfsame measure of forgiveness.[145]

The final key point that 'Attār makes is the necessity of the Prophetic intercession, 'He saw the Prophet, lovely as the moon, / Whose face, Truth's shadow, was the sun at noon.'[146] It is finally the Prophet's intercession that cleanses and restores the sheikh back to faith and Islam, 'I sprinkled on the fortunes of your sheikh / A cleansing dew for intercession's sake - / The dust is laid; sin disappeared before.'[147] Schimmel states that the Prophet for the masses is the great intercessor on the day of Judgement.[148] On the role of the Prophet as an intercessor, Tustarī notes that 'God has made the Emissary the most elevated and the greatest mediator (*wāsita*) between you and Him.'[149]

In this short story 'Attār has incorporated a mine of teachings of the spiritual journey, expressing not only the necessity of love but also the obstacles and dangers upon the way that one needs to be wary of and overcome.

Qushayriya, trans. by Rabia Harris and ed. by Laleh Bakhtiar (Chicago: Kazi Publications, 1997), p. 1.

[144] 'Attār, *Conference*, p. 72.

[145] Muhyīddīn Ibn 'Arabī, *Divine Sayings: The Mishkāt al-Anwār*, trans. by Stephen Hirtenstein and Martin Notcutt (Oxford: Anqa Publishing, 2004), p. 47.

[146] 'Attār, *Conference*, p. 71.

[147] 'Attār, *Conference*, p. 71-72.

[148] Schimmel, *Mystical*, p. 217.

[149] Tustarī, *Tafsīr*, p. xxx.

5 CONCLUSION

What is striking about both of the works is their similarities and agreement. For Spenser, sets the scene in Book One with Arthur's vision of Gloriana, 'whose excellent beauty' becomes the catalyst for his search of her. This is not to be understated, as the power of this vision is such that it 'moves' Arthur's being and is therefore the catalyst for his search of Gloriana. Attār similarly uses exquisite imagery of beauty, of uniqueness and fulfilment, in describing the bird-king Sīmorgh. Although the birds proffer various excuses, they nonetheless are so compelled by the majesty and beauty of the Sīmorgh, that they too begin the journey to self-realisation. Both of the authors utilise these two characters to articulate a multi-layered set of meanings. At one level Gloriana is the Queen but at another deeper level signifies the Divine. Likewise, Sīmorgh is at one level the bird-king but at a deeper level the Divine. This multi-layering of meanings through the allegory enables the authors to draw in, scandalize, transform, and maximise impact upon their respective audiences. Both in their respective ways are seeking to awaken the Christian and Muslim believers by reminding them of that which lies beyond this material existence.

The Redcrosse knight begins his career as an upstart, clownish young man, but his putting on the 'armour of God' of Ephesians 6.11-17 sees a transformation of him into the goodliest man in all the company. The armour, in the light of St Paul's theology is not just the clothing that is put on but it also entails the body, so that both become one in Christ. When Spenser employs the symbolism of the armour with the shield and the cross, he is packing into this symbolism the totality of biblical teaching. The bloody cross is no longer a symbol but is the signifier of the Christ's suffering, crucifixion and resurrection – it becomes through the symbolism of the blood and the cross the taking on by the knight, of a new psychic and spiritual disposition. Significantly, this also points to the spiritual presence of Christ with the Redcrosse knight and the Christian everyman, in the words of Gless, this becomes the 'emblem of the Lord who died once in order to live and send aid to His knights forever.' It is inevitable that this might be a point of difference between 'Aṭṭār and Spenser, for 'Aṭṭār as a Muslim and Ṣūfī, could not accept the Christological interpretation given here. However, the putting on of Christ is for the purpose of protection from evil and that is another point of agreement, so although there is disagreement on the theology, nonetheless there is agreement on where the danger lies.

The armour is the means through which the Christian man can be shielded from the 'assaults of the devil, the flesh, the world, the heat of persecution, and the cold of defection.' In the light of Leslie's elucidation of St Paul's theology, the implications for the body are that it is the 'chief weapon in the armoury of sin and death.' Although, Islam does not hold to a belief of original sin, nonetheless, there are striking similarities about the nature of the lower self. In the treatment of the 'soul commanding evil' 'Aṭṭār highlights the dangers of the lower self or in biblical terms, the flesh. This is the great enemy that the Prophet had alluded to in his tradition on the greater Jihād and that the Muslim must do battle against thereby placing the military enemy at a lower level, than the enemy within ourselves. What is striking is the similarity of the lower self with St Paul's theology of the body. The description in the Qur'ān states that the lower self, commands, incites and tempts the human beings to evil. Al-Jawziyya equates the devil as the companion of the lower self through which he awakens desires, leads to falsehoods and various destructive appetites. Whereas, the Qur'ān aims to reform the self, St Paul takes the view that the self is destroyed through the act of baptism in Christ, 'our old man is crucified with him, that the body of sin might be destroyed.'

We noted that pride was the downfall of the Redcrosse knight as it was his pursuit of his desire for fame and pride that were a hindrance to him achieving genuine spiritual growth. His reform in the house of Holiness is necessary and after his instruction by *Fidelia*, he is overcome with the sense of his wicked ways leading to genuine remorse and repentance.

Repentance or *tawba* is another point of similarity. 'Aṭṭār states, 'The sea of righteousness drowns in its waves / The sins of those sincere repentance saves', on the importance and spiritual significance of a genuine renewal of spiritual growth. We noted that for al-Qushayrī repentance was the first step on the spiritual path and as human beings are always likely to fall short and sin, this is the means through which they might seek forgiveness. 'Aṭṭār effectively provides a commentary on sin through his story of Sheikh Sam'ān and demonstrates that God's forgiveness is always greater than his wrath; despite the sheikh having transgressed all the limits of the law, he is forgiven and here is another point of similarity between the two works.

Whereas the 'armour of God' signifies to the Redcrosse knight his relationship with Christ and his helping hand through the aid of Una and Arthur, who both to various degrees it can be argued, represent Christ. Likewise, it is the mediation of the Prophet that is the catalyst for the restoration of Sheikh Sam'ān. 'Attār here is pointing to the perfection of the Prophet as the Perfect Man and the great mediator between heaven and earth, between God and His creation.

'Attār and Spenser deploy symbols, allusions, and characters in their masterpieces to show both the ultimate end of human journeying but also the dangers that lurk on the way, as well as the preparedness required for a successful end. They both demonstrate the susceptibility of human beings to the machinations of the lower self or 'the flesh'. However, despite the challenges and battles to be fought within, with temptation, desires of all sorts, pride, vanity and falsehood, to name a few, the mercy of God is at hand.

At a time in the world when politicians and some religious leaders speak of confrontation between Christians and Muslims, we must remind them that what we have in common is far greater than that which divides us. Our focus, as people of faith, should be the perfection our own selves, within and without, by doing so we will have no enemies to conquer but see around us our brothers and sisters, either in humanity or in faith.

BIBLIOGRAPHY

Akbari, Suzanne Conklin, 'The rhetoric of antichrist in Western lives of Muhammad', *Islam and Christian-Muslim Relations*, 8 (1997), 297-307.

al-'Arabī, Ibn, *Sufis of Andalusia: The Rūh al-Quds and Al-Durrat al Fākhirah* (Sherborne: Beshara Publications, 1971).

al-'Arabī, Ibn, *Whoso Knoweth Himself...*, trans. by The Muhyiddīn Ibn 'Arabī Society (Abingdon: Beshara Publications, 1988).

al-'Arabī, Ibn, *The Meccan Revelations*, ed. by Michel Chodkiewicz (New York: Pir Press, 2002).

al-'Arabī, Ibn, *Divine Sayings: The Mishkāt al-Anwār*, trans. by Stephen Hirtenstein and Martin Notcutt (Oxford: Anqa Publishing, 2004).

Abdel-Kader, Ali Hassan, *The Life, Personality and Writings of Al-Junayd*, (London: Luzac & Company Ltd, 1976).

Asceric-Todd, Ines, 'The Noble Traders: The Islamic Tradition of "Spiritual Chivalry" (*futuwwah*) in Bosnian Trade-guilds (16th-19th centuries)', *The Muslim World*, 7 (2007), 159-173.

Asín, Miguel, *Islam and The Divine Comedy*, trans. by Harold Sutherland (New Delhi: Goodword Books, 2002).

'Attār, Farīd ud-Dīn, *The Conference of the Birds*, trans. by Afkham Darbandi and Dick Davies (London: Penguin Books, 1984).

Bergvall, Åke, 'The Theology of the Sign: St Augustine and Spenser's Legend of Holiness', *Studies in English Literature*, 33 (1993), 21-42.

Bonomi, Bianca Brigitte, 'Seeing, Believing, and Anti-Catholicism in Book One of Spenser's *Faerie Queene*', *Reformation & Renaissance Review: Journal of the Society for Reformation Studies*, 7 (2005), 163-187.

Brink, Jean R., 'Revising Edmund Spenser's Birth Date to 1554', *Notes & Queries*, 56 (2009), 523-527.

Broaddus, James W., 'Spenser's Redcrosse Knight and the Order of Salvation', *Studies in Philology*, 108 (2011), 572-604.

Bruijn, de, J. T. P., 'Comparative Notes on Sanāʾī and ʿAttār', in *The Heritage of Sufism: Classical Persian Sufism from its Origins to Rumi (700-1300)*, ed. by Leonard Lewisohn (Oxford: Oneworld, 1999), pp. 361-380.

Carter, Ronald and John McRae, *The Routledge History of English Literature* (London: Routledge, 2001), p. 55.

Council, Norman, 'Ben Jonson, Inigo Jones, and the Transformation of Tudor Chivalry', *ELH*, 47 (1980), 259-275.

DeMoss, William Fenn, 'Spenser's Twelve Moral Virtues "According to Aristotle"', *Modern Philology*, 16 (1918), 23-38.

Doyle, Charles Clay, 'Christian Vision in *The Faerie Queene*, Book 1', *College Literature*, 3 (1976), 33-41

Dupree, Nancy Hatch, 'An interpretation of the Role of the Hoopoe in Afghan Folklore and Magic', *Folklore*, 3 (1974), 173-193.

DuRoucher, Richard J., 'Arthur's Gift, Aristotle's Magnificence, and Spenser's Allegory: A Study of "Faerie Queene" 1.9.19', *Modern Philology*, 82 (1984), 185-190.

Ernst, Carl W., *Sufism: An Essential Introduction to the Philosophy and Practice of the Mystical Tradition of Islam* (Boston: Shambhala Publications, 1997).

Evans, Maurice, *Spenser's Anatomy of Heroism: A Commentary on The Faerie Queene* (Cambridge: Cambridge University Press, 1970).

Feinstein, Blossom, 'The Faerie Queene and Cosmogonies of the Near East', *Journal of History of Ideas*, 29 (1968), 531-550

Fike, Matthew A., 'Prince Arthur and Christ's descent into Hell: *The Faerie Queene*, I.viii and II.viii', *ANQ* 12 (1999), 6-14.

Friemuth, Maha Elkaisy, 'Allegory', in *Encyclopedia of the Bible and Its Reception* (Berlin, Boston: De Gruyter, 2010), pp. 807-808.

Frye, Northrop, 'The Structure of Imagery in The Faerie Queene', in *Essential Articles for the study of Edmund Spenser*, ed. by A. C. Hamilton (Connecticut: Archon Books, 1972), pp. 153-170.

al-Ghazālī, *The Ninety-Nine Beautiful Names of God: al-Maqsad al-asnā fī sharh asmā'Allāh al-husnā*, trans. by David B. Burrell and Nazih Daher (Cambridge: Islamic Text Society, 1995).

al-Ghazālī, *On Disciplining the Soul and Breaking the Two Desires: Books XXII and XXIII of The Revival of the Religious Sciences*, trans. by T. J. Winter (Cambridge: Islamic Texts Society, 2001).

Gless, Darryl J., *Interpretation and Theology in Spenser* (Cambridge: Cambridge University Press, 1994).

Hadfield, Andrew, 'Spenser, Ireland, and Sixteenth-Century Political Theory', in *The Modern Language Review*, Vol. 89, 1 (1994), pp. 1-18.

Hadfield, Andrew, 'Spenser, Edmund (1552?-1599)', in *Oxford Dictionary of National Biography*, http://dx.doi.org/10.1093/ref:odnb/26145.

Hadfield, Andrew, *Edmund Spenser's Irish Experience: Wilde Fruit and Salvage Soyl* (Oxford: Oxford Scholarship Online, 2011). http://dx.doi.org/10.1093/acprof:oso/9780198183457.001.0001. Online book.

Hagen, Kenneth, 'Allegory', in *Encyclopedia of the Bible and Its Reception* (Berlin: De Gruyter, 2010), 800-802.

Hamilton, A. C., 'Spenser's "Letter to Ralegh"', *Modern Language Notes*, 73 (1958), 481-485.

Hankins, John Erskine, *Source and Meaning in Spenser's Allegory: A Study of The Faerie Queene* (Oxford: The Clarendon Press, 1971).

Haylamaz, Resit, *Ali Ibn Abi Talib: The Hero of Chivalry* (New Jersey: Tughra Books, 2011).

Heer, Nicholas, 'Abū Hamīd al-Ghazālī's Esoteric Exegesis of the Koran', in *The Heritage of Sufism: Classical Persian Sufism from its Origins to Rumi (700-1300)* ed. by Leonard Lewisohn (Oxford: Oneworld, 1999), pp. 235-258.

al-Hujwīrī, 'Alī b. 'Uthmān al-Jullābī, *Kashf al-Mahjūb: The Revelation of the Veiled*, trans. by Reynold A. Nicholson (Warminster: E. J. W. Gibb Memorial Trust, 2000).

Jusserand, J. J. 'Spenser's "Twelve Private Morall Vertues as Aristotle Hath Devised"', *Modern Philology*, 3 (1906), 373-383.

Kabbani, Shaykh Muhammad Hisham, *Self-purification and the State of Excellence* (California: As-Sunna Foundation of America, 1998).

Kaske, Carol V., 'The Dragon's Spark and Sting and the Structure of Red Cross's Dragon-Fight: The Faerie Queene, I.xi-xii', in *Essential Articles for the study of Edmund Spenser*, ed. by A. C. Hamilton (Connecticut: Archon Books, 1972), pp. 425-446.

Khalil, Atif, 'Abū Tālib al-Makkī & the Nourishment of Hearts (*Qūt al-qulūb*) in the Context of Early Sufism', *The Muslim World*, 102 (2012), 335-356.

King James Bible <http://www.kingjamesbibleonline.org/Ephesians-Chapter-6/> [accessed 12th August 2016].

Konstan, David and Ilaria Ramelli, 'Allegory', in *Encyclopedia of the Bible and Its Reception*, <http://www.degruyter.com/view/db/ebr> [accessed 28 August 2016].

Leslie, Michael, *Spenser's 'Fierce Warres and Faithfull Loves': Martial and Chivalric Symbolism in 'The Faerie Queene'* (Cambridge: D. S. Brewer, 1983).

Lewis, C. S., *English Literature in the Sixteenth Century Excluding Drama* (Oxford: OUP, 1973).

Lings, Martin, *The Secret of Shakespeare: His Greatest Plays Seen in the Light of Sacred Art* (Cambridge: Quinta Essentia, 1996).

Mahjub, Muhammad Ja'far, 'Chivalry and Early Persian Sufism', in *The Heritage of Sufism: Classical Persian Sufism from its Origins to Rumi (700-1300)*, ed. by Leonard Lewisohn (Oxford: Oneworld, 1999), p. 551-553.

Manion, Lee, *Narrating the Crusades: Loss and Recovery in Medieval and Early Modern English Literature* (Cambridge: Cambridge University Press, 2014), p. 146. <http://dx.doi.org/10.1017/CBO9781107415218>

Masood, Hafiz Abid, 'Islam in Medieval and Early Modern English Literature: A Select Bibliography', *Islamic Studies*, 44 (2005), 553-629.

Matar, Nabil, 'Britons and Muslims in the early modern period: from prejudice to (a theory of) toleration', *Patterns of Prejudice*, 43 (2009), 213-231.

Maybudī, Rashīd al-Dīn, *The Unveiling of the Mysteries and the Provision of the Pious*, trans. by William C. Chittick (Amman: RABIIT, 2014).

Mitchell, Margaret M., 'Allegory', in *Encyclopedia of the Bible and Its Reception* (Berlin: De Gruyter, 2010), 793-800.

Moloney, Michael F., 'St. Thomas and Spenser's Virtue of Magnificence', *The Journal of English and Germanic Philology*, 52 (1953), 58-62.

Morgan, Gerald, 'Holiness as the First of Spenser's Aristotelian Moral Virtues', *The Modern Language Review*, 81 (1986), 817-837.

Morgan, Gerald, 'Add faith vnto your force': the perfecting of Spenser's knight of holiness in faith and humility', *Renaissance Studies*, 18 (2004), 449-474.

Morris, James Winston, 'Reading the Conference of the Birds', in *Approaches to the Asian Classics*, ed. by William Theodore De Bary and Irene Bloom (New York: Columbia University Press, 1990), pp. 77-85.

Morris, Rosemary A., review of *King Arthur: Hero and Legend*, by Richard Barber, *A Quarterly Journal Concerned with British Studies*, 19 (1987), 588-590.

Murrin, Michael, 'The Audience of The Faerie Queene', *Explorations in Renaissance Culture*, 23 (1997), 1-21.

Paolucci, Anne, 'Women in the Political Love-Ethic of the *Divine Comedy* and the *Faerie Queene*,' *Dante Studies, with Annual Report of the Dante Society*, 90 (1972), 139-153.

Pendergast, John S., 'Christian Allegory and Spenser's "General Intention"', *Studies in Philology*, 93 (1996), 267-287.

Picken, Gavin, 'Tazkiyat al-nafs: The Qur'anic Paradigm', *Journal of Qur'anic Studies*, 7 (2005), 101-127.

al-Qushayri, Abu'l-Qasim, *Sufi Book of Spiritual Ascent: Al-Risala Al-Qushayriya*, trans. by Rabia Harris and ed. by Laleh Bakhtiar (Chicago: Kazi Publications, 1997).

al-Razzāq, 'Abd, *Tafsīr al-Kāshānī*, trans. by Feras Hamza (Amman: RABIIT, 2012).

Ritter, H., 'Attār', in *Encyclopaedia of Islam, Second Edition*, <http://referenceworks.brillonline.com/entries/encyclopaedia-of-islam-2/attar-COM_0074> [accessed 21 August 2016].

Robinson, Benedict S., *Islam and Early Modern Literature: The Politics of Romance from Spenser to Milton* (Palgrave Milton, 2007), [e-book], <http://0-www.myilibrary.com.catalogue.libraries.london.ac.uk?ID=173721> [accessed on 30 August 2016].

Schimmel, Annemarie, *Mystical Dimensions of Islam* (Chapel Hill: The University of North Carolina Press, 1975).

Sévère, Richard, 'Galahad, Percival, and Bors: Grail Knights and the Quest for *Spiritual Friendship*', *Arthurian*, 25 (2015), 49-65.
Spenser, Edmund, *The Faerie Queene*, ed. by A.C. Hamilton (Harlow: Pearson Education, 2007).

Sabzawārī, Husayn Wā'iz Kāshifī, *The Royal Book of Spiritual Chivalry*, trans. by Jay R. Cook (Chicago: Kazi Publications, 2000).

al-Sulamī, Ibn al-Husayn *The way of Sufi Chivalry*, trans. by Tosun Bayrak al-Jerrahi (Vermont: Inner Traditions International, 1991).

Tosello, Mathew, 'Spenser's Silence about Dante', *Studies in English Literature, 1500-1900*, 17(1977), 59-66.

al-Tustarī, Sahl b. 'Abd Allāh, *Tafsīr al-Tustarī*, trans. by Annabel Keeler and Ali Keeler (Louisville: Fons Vitae, 2011).

Valiuddin, Mir, *Contemplative Disciplines in Sufism*, ed. by Gulshan Khakee (London: East-West Publication, 1980).

Vitkus, Daniel J., 'Turning Turk in Othello: the conversion and damnation of the Moor', *Shakespeare Quarterly*, 48 (1997), 145-176.

William Montgomery Watt, *The Faith and Practice of Al-Ghazāli*, (Oxford: Oneworld, 1998).

Whitaker, Virgil K., 'The Theological Structure of The Faerie Queene, Book I', in *Essential Articles for the study of Edmund Spenser*, ed. by A. C. Hamilton (Connecticut: Archon Books, 1972), pp. 101-112.

Wilcox, Andrew, 'The Dual Mystical Concepts of *Fanā'* and *Baqā* in Early Sūfism', *British Journal of Middle Eastern Studies*, 38 (2011), 95-118.

Yaghoobi, Claudia, 'Subjectivity in 'Attār's Shaykh of San'ān Story in The Conference of the Birds', *CLCWeb: Comparative Literature and Culture*, 16.1 (2014), 1-10. <http://dx.doi.org/10.7771/1481-4374.2425>

Zwanzig, Rebekah, 'Why must God Show himself in Disguise? An Exploration of Sufism within Farid Attar's "The Conference of the Birds"', in *Studies on Themes and Motifs in Literature: Disguise, Deception, Trompe-L'oeil: Interdisciplinary Perspectives*, ed. by Leslie Boldt, Corrado Federici and Virgulti Ernesto (New York: Peter Lang, 2008). pp. 273-284. ProQuest.

Online Qur'ānic translations of Marmaduke Pickthall at <www.altafsir.com>

ABOUT THE AUTHOR

Imam Monawar Hussain is the Muslim Tutor at Eton College, Windsor; Muslim Chaplain to the Oxford University Hospitals NHS Foundation Trust and the Founder of The Oxford Foundation.

Imam Monawar read Theology at the University of Oxford, majoring in Islam and the West. He trained as an Imam under the tutelage of the late Sheikh Dr Zaki Badawi KBE at the Muslim College, Ealing, United Kingdom. He also holds a Master of Arts degree in Abrahamic Religions awarded by the University of London. His research interests include Islam and the West, Interfaith dialogue, Islamic reform movements, Sufism and English literature.

Imam Monawar is also an Honorary Research Fellow at the University of Birmingham.

www.theoxfordfoundation.com

https://www.facebook.com/TheOxfordFoundation/

https://www.facebook.com/communitiesunitedagainstextremism/

Email: info@theoxfordfoundation.org.uk

Printed in Great Britain
by Amazon